Ernane R. Martins

Robocode Platform as a Programming Teaching Tool

Ernane R. Martins

Robocode Platform as a Programming Teaching Tool

Using the Robocode Tool to Learn Programming Languages

ScienciaScripts

Imprint

Cover image: www.ingimage.com

This book is a translation from the original published under ISBN 978-3-330-75610-6.

Publisher:
Sciencia Scripts
is a trademark of
Dodo Books Indian Ocean Ltd. and OmniScriptum S.R.L publishing group

120 High Road, East Finchley, London, N2 9ED, United Kingdom
Str. Armeneasca 28/1, office 1, Chisinau MD-2012, Republic of Moldova, Europe
Printed at: see last page
ISBN: 978-620-8-29008-5

SUMMARY

INTRODUCTION

A problem faced by several countries, including Brazil, is the high dropout and failure rates in computer science courses (DIAS; SERRAO, 2014). Student dropout in higher education is a problem that affects the outcome of educational systems, causing social, academic and economic waste. Dropouts are a source of idleness for teachers, staff, equipment and physical space (LOBO ROBERTO, 2007).

According to Freitas and Piva Jr (2011), based on data from the Anisio Teixeira National Institute for Educational Studies and Research (INEP), only 35.1% of the 40,435 students who entered computer science courses in Brazil in 2008 managed to complete their courses.

Currently at several universities, such as the Federal University of Pernambuco and the University of Information Technology in Copenhagen, various ways are being used to facilitate teaching and learning (TE) in educational environments, such as the use of educational games. One of the main tasks facing educators is to motivate students to perform to their best ability. One method of motivating students is game-based exercises (AMARAL et al, 2015; MORAN, 2009; MORAN, 2005; SAVI; ULBRICHT, 2008).

In the field of computing, it is common for students to have difficulties in programming subjects, which is an obstacle to be overcome (LONG, 2007). One of the difficulties of learning programming lies in the fact that it is necessary to learn various concepts in a short space of time and develop specific skills such as abstraction and computational thinking (BITTENCOURT et al., 2013).

Moran et al (2007, p. 11) state that classes based on the expository method, where the teacher is the retainer of knowledge and the student is the receiver, are outdated. Education for the 21st century must be designed for 21st century students (FRANÇA et al., 2013). Classes should aim to use innovative and transformative teaching methodologies, focusing on the search for student participation and interest and the integration of theory and practice (AMARAL, 2004; MORAN, 2005). In this process, the teacher continues to play a fundamental role, not as a transmitter of knowledge, but as a mediator in accessing and organizing processes (MORAN, 2009).

Combining educational content with the fun and excitement of a game makes for an excellent educational tool (AMARAL et al, 2015). Digital media represent a significant transformation in the way young people learn and produce knowledge, i.e. used appropriately, games, competitions and challenges make it possible to increase motivation for learning and make the learning process light and enjoyable. The use of competitions makes activities more exciting for students, leading them to break down their own barriers in the learning process (SANTOS et al, 2015; MATTAR, 2010).

Student dropout is an international problem that affects the results of educational systems. It is common for students to start but not finish courses, whether at technical or higher education level, generating social, academic and economic waste (LOBO ROBERTO, 2007).

The use of games in the teaching environment can become an excellent tool in the learning process, preventing students from dropping out, by helping them to understand not only programming techniques, but also the interaction between students. Educational games help to restore students' self-esteem and confidence, and strengthen the bonds of trust between them and their teachers, as well as between their classmates (NICOLETTI; FILHO, 2004).

Motivating students to pursue their best skills has been one of the main difficulties faced by educators. Thus, the use of computer games becomes a means of support and encouragement in the teaching and learning process (LONG, 2007).

According to Mattar (2010), digital media, including digital games, should be part of the school environment, because the motivation, engagement and immersion with which this generation interacts with digital media outside school needs to be the same as that with which students interact with the syllabus of school subjects.

According to Kapp (2012), gamification is "the use of game mechanics, aesthetics and thinking to engage people, motivate action, promote learning and solve problems". Thus, the use of games in the teaching environment can help with the teaching and learning of certain content.

One of the biggest problems facing Brazilian institutions is the high dropout rate. According to data published on the "todos pela educaçâo" portal, around 10% of students dropped out of secondary school in the public network in 2012, which represents 760,000 students (TPE, 2014).

It should be noted that subjects related to programming languages are one of the main reasons for dropouts and failures in computer science courses (CABRAL, 2007). According to Silveira and Esmin (2003), certain subjects are difficult to assimilate because they are abstract, complex or even tiring, as is the case with web programming.

The use of games in the teaching environment can help with the assimilation of certain content. According to Karl Kapp (2012), gamification is "the use of game mechanics, aesthetics and thinking to engage people, motivate action, promote learning and solve problems".

Improving learning effectiveness has been a constant challenge in education. One of the main difficulties that educators face is motivating students to pursue their best skills. Thus, the use of computer games becomes a means of support and encouragement in the teaching and learning process (LONG, 2007).

According to Mattar (2010), digital media, including digital games, should be part of the school environment, because the motivation, engagement and immersion with which this generation interacts with digital media outside school needs to be the same as that with which students interact with the syllabus of school subjects.

Robocode was chosen as the tool of study because of the references found in various works such as Woolley and Peterson (2009), Harper (2011), O'Kelly and Gibson (2006), Liu (2008), Bonakdarian and White (2004).

Therefore, Robocode can be used as a tool that stimulates the learning of Object-Oriented Programming, creativity, participation in group work, the learning of notions of physics and geometry, puts into practice what has been studied and approached in the classroom, stimulates creativity and the acceptance of new challenges, explores teamwork and competitiveness (MARTINS, 2015).

This paper aims to describe an experience of using the Robocode tool to support the teaching of programming, in order to stimulate interest in programming subjects.

In terms of methodology, this work consisted of descriptive research, as it described the opinions of certain groups, field research to collect data through questionnaires, and bibliographical research, as it used information from books and technical and academic publications.

The article is organized into the following sections. In addition to this introduction. Section 1 reviews the literature and provides a conceptual and theoretical basis for understanding the main concepts discussed. Section 2 deals with the methodology, in which the methodological procedures used in the research are presented. Section 3 presents the results achieved and the experience with the project, which strongly suggest that Robocode can be effective in promoting the learning of programming. Finally, final considerations and prospects for future work are presented.

1. THEORETICAL FRAMEWORK

According to Martins (2014), Robocode is a programming game, where the objective is to develop a robot battle tank to battle other tanks in a virtual arena using the Java programming language. So, as well as being a programming game, Robocode is also used to learn how to program. Schools and universities are using Robocode to help teach programming as well as to study artificial intelligence (AI), through its class library. The concept of Robocode is easy to understand, and a fun way to learn to program.

In Robocode, the programmer has to choose the best strategy for his robot, being able to manipulate events that occur during the fight, such as avoiding hitting a wall or dodging his opponent's bullets. The battles between the robots consist of one or several rounds, in which the robots start from a random starting position and have to fight each other, individually or in teams (MARTINS, 2015).

Users of the environment have access to an introductory tutorial and a complete Robocode API. The system integrates an editor and compiler as part of the Robocode environment. A template for new robot tanks is provided (BONAKDARIAN; WHITE, 2004).

In Robocode, robots battle to the death in an arena. The battle consists of a predetermined number of rounds, with the winner of the battle being the robot with the most points. The round ends when only one robot remains from that round. The robots start with an energy level of 100 and die when the energy level drops below zero. The robots are equipped with radar, which can scan other robots up to 1200 pixels away. The radar returns information about the robot, such as distance, position, speed, name and energy (GADE, 2003).

The robot consists of a body, radar and gun, each of which can rotate 360 degrees independently of each other. The gun can fire with variable power and heats up when it is fired. A robot has to wait for the gun to cool down before another shot can be fired, and the bullet travels faster when fired with low power consumption. If two robots collide, both lose 0.6 energy points. All battles take place in a rectangular arena of varying size. The standard size is 800 × 600 pixels, while the robots have a size of 36 × 45 pixels. The maximum speed of a robot is 8 pixels per second (GADE, 2003).

During the game, the robot must navigate around the environment, avoiding walls, bullets fired by tanks and other tanks. At the same time, it must locate the other tank and anticipate its likely position. Programs with simple strategies are provided as a sample, to help the novice programmer get started with Robocode. In addition, there are several resources on the internet illustrating advanced strategies (HARPER, 2011).

Robots are created as a new Java class. Robot objects have an execute method with an infinite loop that describes the standard behavior for the robot. In addition, other methods are invoked in response to events. Responses include commands such as ahead(distance), back(distance), turnLeft(degrees), turnRight(degrees), fire(strength), turnGunLeft(degrees), among others (HARTNESS, 2004, KENSLER; AGAH, 2009).

In the Robocode environment, as shown in Figure 1, it is possible to create an arena and configure the battle by adding the robots.

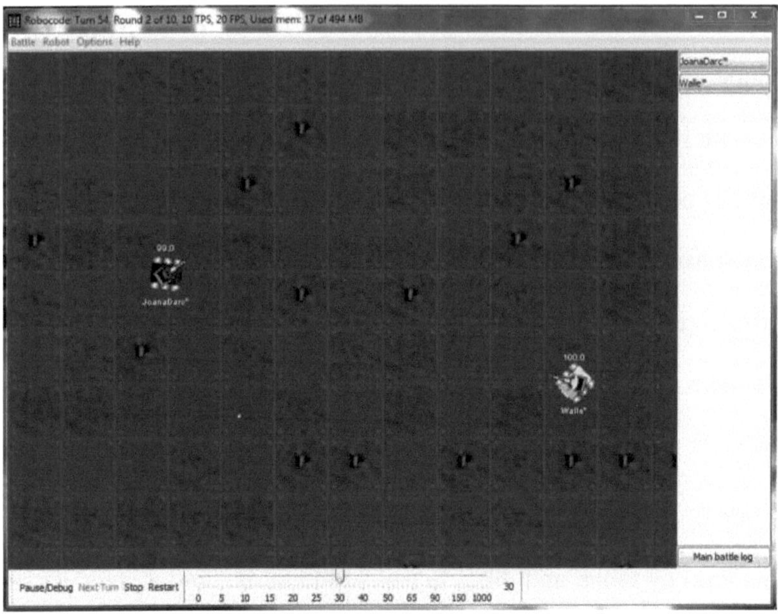

Figure 1 - Main screen of the Robocode virtual environment

Source: Own.

Interactivity with the user is programmed through events for handling the mouse and keyboard. In addition, there are events to warn the robot when it hits an opponent or is hit, when it is eliminated from the battle, or when it is finished (LIMA et al, 2014).

The environment contains its own source code editor for programming the robots, as shown in Figure 2.

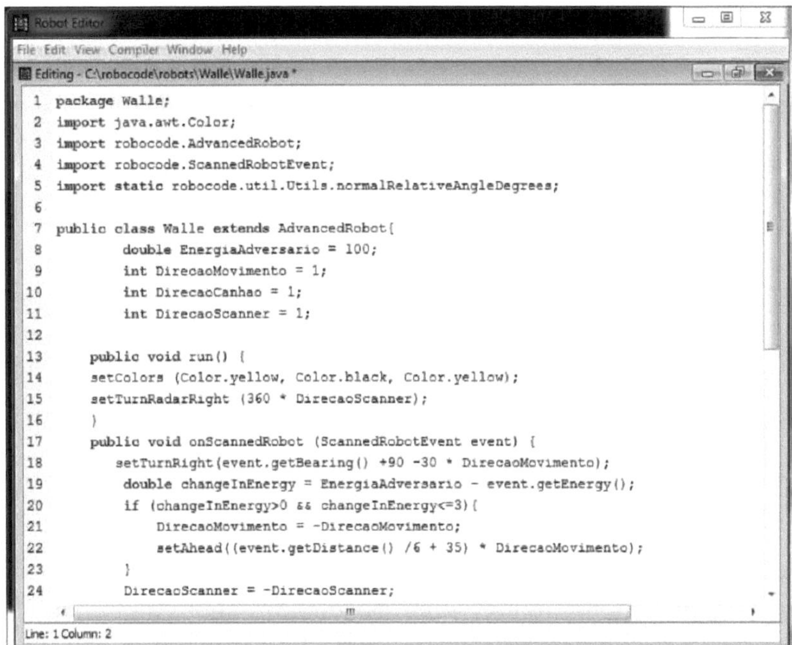

Figure 2 - Robocode source code editor

Source: Own.

The logic of the robots in Robocode is concentrated in methods, which define the actions and movements of the robots. In addition, robot movement and some actions, such as shooting at other robots, are based on the definition of pre-specified angles, i.e. requiring the direct application of mathematical concepts. You can change: the direction of rotation of the robot and the gun, which can be moved to the right or left, individually or together; the direction of movement, which can be forward or backward; as well as the characteristics of the bullet, which can change its firepower, direction and speed (AMARAL et al, 2015).

There are several works on Robocode in the literature, such as:

- Czajkowski and Patan (2009), who reported on turret control tasks in Robocode agents. This involves trying to predict the enemy's position from their last positions in order to fire.
- Liu (2008), who described an experience of using Robocode for three weeks with 26 undergraduate students. He reports that the use of Robocode portrays realistic situations, which motivates the participants. It also reports that the need for exploration and self-learning is very present in the students' reports.
- O'KELLY and GIBSON (2006) used Problem-Based Learning (PBL), applied to undergraduate students, with the aim of developing battles with the robots implemented by the students in order to portray reality in a competitive professional environment. To this end, teams were set up, as it is common to program in pairs. The winners took part in a national battle, motivating the students' competitive spirit. The PBL methodology emphasizes self-directed, student-centered learning.
- Amarai, Silva and Pantaleâo (2015) describe the experience of using the Robocode tool to teach algorithms and computer programming to high school students. The study also involved undergraduate students who had already studied computer programming and who acted as tutors and co-supervisors for the students. The Robocode environment was used as a tool to support the teaching of algorithms and programming languages, based on a playful

teaching strategy, suggesting earlier contact with the Java programming language, while still in high school, in order to stimulate the logical-mathematical reasoning of those involved in a fast and fun way. In addition to the students learning to program computers, the results observed include an increase in interest in programming among high school students and the development of leadership skills among undergraduates, stemming from the experience of co-supervising student apprentices.

- Martins (2015) presents Robocode as a tool that can help with the teaching and learning of the Web Programming I and II subjects in the Internet Computer Technician course. In order to achieve the objective, a Robocode championship was organized and held, followed by a survey of the students in relation to the activity carried out. Finally, it presents the results found, which strongly suggest that Robocode can be effective in promoting the learning of Object-Oriented Programming, with more than 90% of the participants reporting that their programming skills had increased as a result of taking part in the Robocode championship. It was also noted that the average grade in the Web Programming I subject went up from 4.1 to 7.2 compared to the grades in the subject in the previous year when Robocode was not used.

- Silva and Nascimento (2012) present the initial results of a research project that aims to investigate new techniques for improving learning through experimentation. The project aims to review the literature, administer workshops and questionnaires, apply practical tests and analyze the data obtained. The aim is to prove that the use of programming, robotics and games such as RoboMind and RoboCode are beneficial to the learning process and that they can be used as an auxiliary learning tool.

- Santos et al. (2015) report on an experience with Object-Oriented Programming (OOP) learning workshops through games, challenges and competitions supported by the Greenfoot and Robocode tools, with second-year students on a Computer Engineering course. The experience highlighted important lessons for motivating students: the development of good examples, the use of competitive challenges and a good ratio between tutors and participants. In addition, the workshop proved to be practical and effective in introducing and motivating students to learn OOP.

- According to Fardo (2013), gamification is a phenomenon that consists of "the use of elements, strategies and thoughts from games outside the context of a game, in order to contribute to solving a problem".

- The game, according to Batista (2010), "requires structural modes of intelligence from the player in order to relate rules, content, strategies and schemes. In other words, playing requires skills and abilities that allow information and action to be articulated."

Robocode is a programming game where the objective is to develop a battle tank to fight other tanks in a virtual arena, using the Java programming language. Schools and universities are using Robocode to help teach programming as well as to study Artificial Intelligence (AI). Robocode's concepts are easy to understand, making it a fun way to learn to program. As it is free software that runs on the Java platform, it can be run on any operating system with Java installed (ROBOCODE, 2015).

In Robocode, the programmer has to choose the best strategy for his robot and can manipulate events that occur during the fight, such as avoiding hitting a wall or dodging an opponent's bullets. The battles between the robots consist of one or several rounds, in which the robots start from a random starting position and fight each other, individually or in teams (MARTINS, 2014).

With Robocode, students are able to see their robots actually executing the consequences of their commands and calculations on the computer screen. Students are encouraged to master concepts so that they can apply their knowledge in interesting or fun situations (HARTNESS, 2004). According to O'kelly and Gibson (2006), Robocode gives each student the freedom to think for themselves, activate their prior knowledge and acquire new knowledge in an exploratory and creative way.

In the Robocode programming environment, robots can be created, placed in the arena and battles carried out between opponents developed using different techniques. Figure 3 shows the Robocode home screen with its functionalities:

Battle - To create new battles, open files with pre-programmed battles, exit Robocode; Robot - Create new robots or robot teams, package robots, edit your robots and more; Options - Options for displaying robots and battles; Help - lots of help.

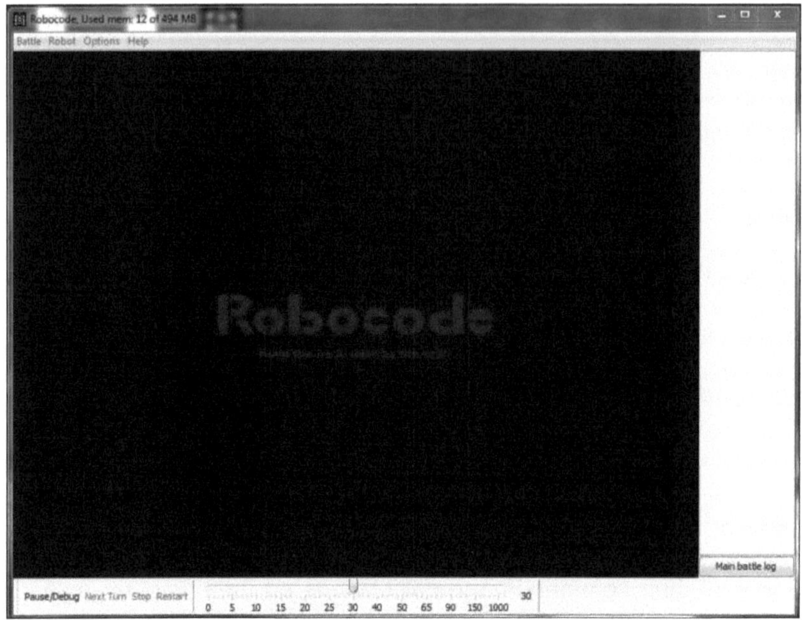

Figure 3 - Robocode home screen

Robocode is used for developers to test their implementations, and they can run simulations against the best implementations developed in various leagues around the world (SILVA, 2007).

New robots can be built in Robocode by extending existing classes such as the Robot class, as shown in Figure 4. Robocode has several example robots and makes it possible to implement complex classes with Artificial Intelligence (AI). Hartness (2004) exemplifies some algorithms in his work, demonstrating the usefulness of the tool in the use and teaching of AI.

```
public class MyFirstRobot extends Robot {

    /**
     * MyFirstRobot's run method - Seesaw
     */
    public void run() {

        while (true) {
            ahead(100); // Move ahead 100
            turnGunRight(360); // Spin gun around
            back(100); // Move back 100
            turnGunRight(360); // Spin gun around
        }
    }

    /**
     * Fire when we see a robot
     */
    public void onScannedRobot(ScannedRobotEvent e) {
        fire(1);
    }

    /**
     * We were hit!  Turn perpendicular to the bullet,
     * so our seesaw might avoid a future shot.
     */
    public void onHitByBullet(HitByBulletEvent e) {
        turnLeft(90 - e.getBearing());
    }
}
```

Figura 4. Robocode example code

Robots are made up of three elements: Cannon (tower), Radar and chassis (wheels), each with independent movements.

The objects contain a main method that loops and describes the robot's standard behavior. In addition, the robot has other methods to invoke in response to events that occur during the battle simulation. These events make it possible to check the distance from the opponent, the angle of movement, the angle of the weapons, the power of the weapons, among others (KENSLER; AGAH, 2009).

Figure 5 shows the running screen of the Robocode tool in the battle between the JoanaDarc and Walle robots, first and second respectively in the second edition of the Robocode championship.

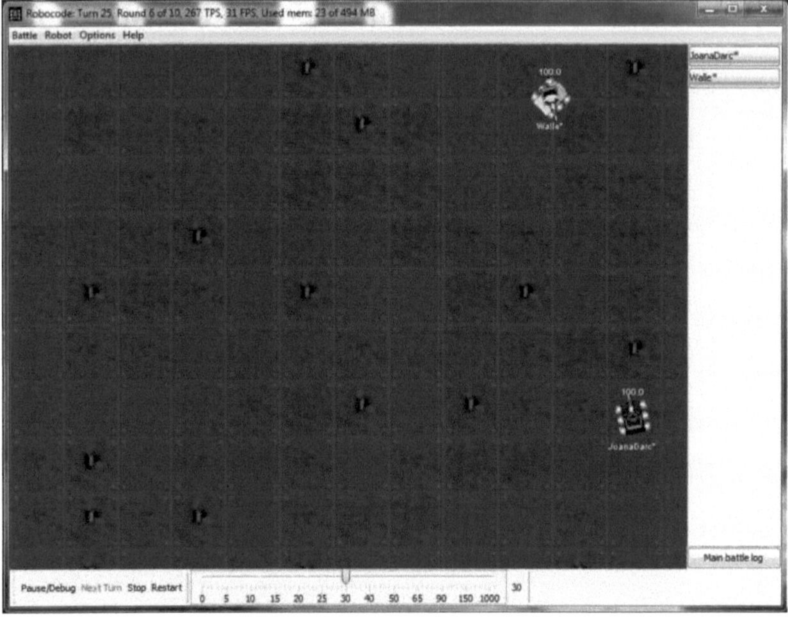

Figura 5. Robocode environment

Each robot starts a battle with 100 energy points and is destroyed as soon as these points reach zero. The weapon used by the robots consists of a turret that can be moved at 360° angles. The power of the gun has different levels, one with higher power and lower speed and the other with lower power and higher speed. The shots also have another effect on the agents, as the projectiles work on a reward system in which successes give life to the robot that fired the shot and errors cause it to lose life points (GADE et al, 2003).

By bringing the game closer to the context of education, Wideman et al. (2007) point out that its use enhances the understanding of complex concepts "without losing the connections between real problems and the abstract ideas that can be used to solve them".

The game helps the student to build knowledge and values about the challenges and issues presented, developing and enriching their personality, and also places the teacher in the position of mediator, stimulator and evaluator of learning (Cunha, 2012).

In this context, it can be seen that the greatest desire in using games as teaching tools is to engage people in the same goal, through healthy competition that generates more and more motivation.

Robocode is a programming game, where the objective is to develop a robot battle tank for battle against other tanks in a virtual arena using the Java programming language. So, as well as being a game, Robocode is also used to learn how to program. Schools and universities are using Robocode to help teach programming as well as to study artificial intelligence (AI). Robocode's concepts are easy to understand, making it a fun way to learn to program (ROBOCODE, 2014).

Robocode comes with its own Java editor and compiler, and only requires the

Java Virtual Machine (JVM) to be previously installed. The fact that Robocode runs on the Java platform makes it possible to run it on any Java operating system (ROBOCODE, 2014).

In Robocode, the programmer has to choose the best strategy for their robot and can manipulate events that occur during the fight, such as avoiding hitting a wall or dodging their opponent's bullets. The battles between the robots consist of one or several rounds, in which the robots start from a random starting position and have to fight each other, individually or in teams.

With Robocode, students are able to see their objects visually performing their activities, or at least the consequences of their commands and calculations on the computer screen. These students are encouraged to master difficult concepts so that they can apply their knowledge in interesting or fun situations (HARTNESS, 2004). According to O'Kelly and Gibson (2006), Robocode gives each student the freedom to think for themselves, activate their prior knowledge and acquire new knowledge in an exploratory and creative way.

Figure 6 shows the running screen of the Robocode tool in the battle between the robots Walle and Ebola, first and second respectively in the Robocode championship held at the Federal Institute of Goiás Luziânia campus.

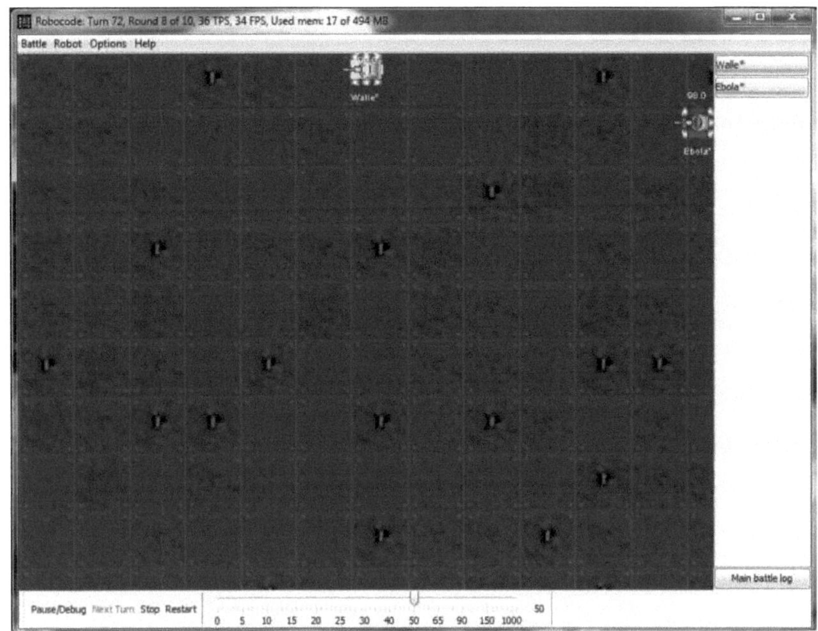

Figure 6. Robocode environment.

2. METHODOLOGY

The research method adopted was a case study. Yin (2005) says that a case study is a type of empirical research that investigates a contemporary phenomenon within its real-life context.

According to Yin (2005) the case study is the preferred strategy when "how" and "why" questions are asked, when the investigator has little control over the events and when the focus is on a contemporary phenomenon in some real-life context.

This paper presents the experiences of the Robocode championships held at the Federal Institute of Goiás in 2015 and 2016. The events were held successfully.

For the championships, notices were made available with information such as: objectives, registration form, delivery of robots, championship rules, prizes and timetable.

The championships were held as a complementary activity lasting eight hours, with the participation of students from the higher education course in Information Systems and students from the technical course in internet computing at the Federal Institute of Goiás Luziânia campus.

Two weeks before the Robocode championships, two-hour Robocode mini-courses were offered and held at the Software Freedom Day events, given by the teacher of the subjects involved, with the aim of introducing and teaching the participating students how to prepare their robots for the competition.

At the end of the competitions, interviews were conducted using semi-structured questionnaires. The purpose of the survey was to ascertain the students' opinions of Robocode.

At the end of the events, questionnaires were made available for the students to answer with various questions, including whether the use of the Robocode tool made the Object-Oriented Programming content of the web programming course more attractive, intuitive and easier to learn, on a scale of one to five for evaluation values, where one represents totally disagree and five represents totally agree, and another question aimed specifically at the perception of the effectiveness of students learning new programming skills using Robocode, with the alternatives: increased a lot, increased a little, or stayed the same.

At the end of the championships, each participant was asked to give a free written report in the form of a questionnaire, which was made available to the students, with the following questions: Did you already know about the Robocode platform? Has the activity provided me with new knowledge? Would you like to do this type of activity again and why?

Robocode was chosen as the tool to study because of the references found in various works, such as: Woolley and Peterson (2009), Harper (2011), O'Kelly and Gibson (2006), Liu (2008), Bonakdarian and White (2004), and because it has several relevant aspects, such as: large community of active developers, dissemination of the tool available since 2001, integration with other development IDEs, various basic and advanced tutorials, focus on teaching the Java programming language and relatively easy implementation (GADE *et al*, 2003).

The choice of Robocode as a study tool was also due to its educational value, since students need to create, maintain and improve their programs in order to compete, learning to use the Java programming language and the concepts of object orientation in software development, exploring all the development phases from their algorithms,

implementation, optimization, testing and bug fixing. Another important factor to note is that unlike classroom simulations, Robocode is a real program, with real participants and real rewards (LONG, 2007).

The order in which the teams competed corresponded to the draw that took place the day before the event, and the day after the robots were delivered by the teams. In the first phase, the teams were divided into four groups A, B, C and D. Each team faced the other teams in their group in a three-round battle. Each victory corresponded to one point and a defeat to zero. At the end of the group stage, only the top two teams from each group progressed to the next stage, the quarter-finals. From the quarter-finals onwards, the matches were five rounds. In the second phase, there were four matches that took place as follows : the first-placed team from group A played the second-placed team from group B; the first-placed team from group B played the second-placed team from group A; the first-placed team from group C played the second-placed team from group D; the first-placed team from group D played the second-placed team from group C. The matches in the next phase, the semi-finals, were also five rounds and proceeded as follows: the team that won the first match faced the winner of the second match and the team that won the third match faced the winner of the fourth match. The losing teams in the semi-final played for 3rd place and the winners for 1st and 2nd place.

3. ANALYSIS AND DISCUSSION OF THE RESULTS OBTAINED

This chapter describes the results of the research into the studies carried out and presents an analysis of them.

3.1 ROBOCODE AS A TOOL FOR TEACHING PROGRAMMING IN AN INFORMATION SYSTEMS COURSE

At the end of the last day of the championships, the students answered a questionnaire that assessed its effectiveness in arousing interest or reinforcing students' learning in the Information Systems course, leading them to stay on the course.

Table 1 shows the results of the questions on the form and the percentage responses of the Information Systems undergraduates taking part in the 2015 Robocode championship.

Table 1. Questionnaire with students' answers

QUESTIONS	2015	
	Yes	No
Are you interested in programming through this Robocode championship?	95%	0,5%
Has the Robocode championship made it easier to understand programming?	89%	11%
Did the Robocode championship motivate you to learn more about programming?	92%	0,8%

Did you already know the Robocode software before the Robocode championship?	0,3%	97%
Would you like to see this type of activity carried out again?	100%	0%

Source: Own.

The answers to the questionnaire shown in Table 1 show that more than 90% of the students say that their interest in programming increased after the Robocode championship. More than 80% of the students reported that the Robocode championship made it easier to understand programming. Over 90% of the students say that the Robocode championship motivated them to learn more about programming. Almost 100% of the students say they didn't know the software before the Robocode championship. And all the students who took part in the Robocode championship agree that this activity should be carried out again.

Asked why this activity should be done again. This is how the students put it:

"for students to show off their programming skills".

"because it helps a little in understanding the subject".

"Because it brings the possibility of acquiring new experiences and encourages teamwork."

"because it's a dynamic activity and helps with the subject".

"It's a complementary activity that helps integrate the students."

"because it helps to learn new ways of programming."

"Because this way we add more knowledge to our curriculum. In the academic sphere we are motivated to think, research and be more curious people."

To further confirm the efficiency of the project, the number of students enrolled, students who failed, the percentage of students who failed and students who passed, and the average number of students who passed the programming II course in the previous year in which undergraduates did not take part in the Robocode championship were presented and compared with the same data from 2015 in which undergraduates took part. As shown in Table 2.

Table 2. Percentage of students who passed, failed and class average

Programming II					
A no	Enrolled	Failures	% of failures	Approval %	Class average
2014	17	12	70,58	29,42	3,87
2015	15	7	46,66	53,34	5,93

Source: Own.

According to table 2, more than 70% of the students in the 2014 programming II class failed the subject. On the other hand, in 2015, with the participation of undergraduates in the Robocode championship, failure was less than 50%. This result strongly suggests that Robocode was effective in promoting learning.

The t-test with independent samples was used to compare the means. The t-test is the most widely used statistical method for evaluating differences between the means of two groups. The results obtained with the Action tool are shown in figure 7 below.

Informação	Valor
T	-1,804125482
Graus de Liberdade	4
P-valor	0,145538174
Média no grupo 1:	3,866666667
Média no grupo 2:	5,933333333
Desvio padrão amostral do grupo 1:	1,650252506
Desvio padrão amostral do grupo 2:	1,101514109
Desvio padrão agrupado:	1,402973034
Hipótese Alternativa: Diferente de	0
Intervalo de Confiança	95%
Limite Inferior	-5,247147519
Limite Superior	1,113814185

Figure 7. Results of the t-test with independent samples

Source: Own.

It can be seen in Table 2 and Figure 7 that in the previous year the average grade for programming II (group 1) was 3.87. After taking part in the Robocode championship, the average for the programming II subject (group 2) was 5.93. This further reinforces the suggestion that the Robocode tool applied to promote learning really is effective.

Low academic performance in the programming subject can be one of the main causes of students dropping out of the Information Systems course and being retained in the semester. From this case study, it was possible to see the potential of the Robocode environment as a playful tool to facilitate the teaching-learning process, and it can be used as a tool for teachers who teach this type of subject.

3.2 EXPERIENCE REPORT: USE OF ROBOCODE IN SECONDARY AND HIGHER EDUCATION

The results show the answers to the questions asked by the students taking part in the second Robocode championship. With regard to the first question, did you already know the Robocode platform? The vast majority answered that they did not know it (81%), a small proportion said that they knew it only vaguely (13%), and the rest (6%) said that they already knew the Robocode tool. All the participants also said that the activity had provided them with new knowledge (100%).

With regard to the rating of the activity carried out, more than half said that the activity was excellent (53%), almost all the rest said that the activity was very good (42%), the rest were divided into good (3%) and regular (2%), and no one said that the activity carried out was bad (0%).

When asked if they would like this type of activity to be carried out again and why, they said that they would. This was the opinion of the students in the second year of the technical course in Internet Informatics (Second year), the third year of the technical course in Internet Informatics (Third year) and the Higher Course in Information Systems (Higher):

"Yes, because it's a more fun way to learn programming." (Second year);

"Yes, because it forces students to develop their skills and reasoning." (Second year);

"Yes, to increase everyone's capacity and improve their knowledge." (Second year);

"Yes, because it was great." (Second year);

"Yes, because it's an interesting way of learning." (Second year);

"Yes, because it encourages students to learn." (Second year);

"Yes, so that I can study more and come better prepared for upcoming championships." (Second year);

"Yes, because this type of activity motivates students to study more." (Second year);

"Yes, because it makes it possible to develop codes in a more relaxed and fun way." (Second year);

"Yes, because it's different learning." (Third year);

"Yes, because it provides better learning about programming." (Third year);

"Yes, because it's an interesting experience to see programming in a different light." (Third year);

"Yes, because it's an interactive way of learning." (Third year);

"Yes, it's a good activity, very good for improving logic and strategy techniques." (Third year);

"Yes, it's a different way of learning, leading students to be more participative."

(Third year);

"Yes, because in addition to improving student learning, robocode is a differentiated and dynamic tool." (Third year);

"Yes, because it gives computer science students the opportunity to put into practice everything they've been taught in programming." (Third year);

"Yes, because it allowed high school students to participate together with the computer science class in college. Therefore, the objective of integration between the classes was achieved." (Third year);

"Yes! It really develops the students' creativity, demystifying the idea that programming is impossible and boring." (Third year);

"Yes, for students to show their programming skills." (Superior);

"Yes, because it offers the chance to gain new experiences and encourages teamwork." (Superior);

"Yes, because it's a dynamic activity and helps with the subject." (Superior);

"Yes, because it helps a little in understanding the subject." (Superior);

"Yes. It's a complementary activity that helps integrate high school and college students." (Superior);

"Yes, because it helps to learn new ways of programming." (Superior);

"Yes, because it adds more knowledge to our curriculum. In the academic sphere we are motivated to think, research and be more curious people." (Superior);

It's worth noting that repeated answers containing only "yes" were not submitted, and that some students didn't answer the question. It is also important to note that no one answered that they would not like this type of activity to be carried out again.

The responses revealed that for both the technical course students and the higher education students, the activity helped to integrate high school and higher education students, helped to improve knowledge, served to develop programming skills, motivated students to think, research and be more curious.

Some of the benefits cited only by undergraduates were: teamwork, better understanding of the subject content and adding knowledge to the curriculum. Among the benefits cited only by the technical course students were: the opportunity to put into practice the content taught to students in programming classes, the development of creativity, and the fun, different and interesting way of learning provided by the activity.

As observed by the teacher who proposed the activity, possibly due to their level of maturity, the students on the technical course act in a more relaxed manner while the students on the higher education course are more formal, but both showed a high level of interest and benefited greatly from the activity. As a result, it was found that the activity applied and developed in this article is a tool that can facilitate the teaching and learning of students regardless of their level of education.

3.3 using robocode as a tool for teaching object-oriented

programming in the web programming course

The questionnaires revealed that Robocode can help in the teaching and learning of web programming I and II. Figure 8 shows the result of the sum of each answer from the total of thirty-nine answers from the thirty-nine students taking part in the Robocode championship, regarding the question of whether the use of the Robocode tool has made the Object-Oriented Programming content of the web programming course more attractive, intuitive and easier to learn.

More attractive		
Scale	**Frequency**	**Percentage**
1	**0**	0%
2	1	3%
3	10	26%
4	13	33%
5	15	38%
Total	39	100%

More intuitive		
Scale	**Frequency**	**Percentage**
1	0	0%
2	3	8%
3	8	**21%**
4	15	38%
5	13	33%
Total	39	100%

Easier to learn		
Scale	**Frequency**	**Percentage**
1	0	0%
2	3	8%
3	10	26%
4	12	**31%**
5	14	36%
Total	39	100%

Figure 8. Quantitative result of each answer

The results of the survey shown in figure 8 suggest that Robocode was an effective tool, with the vast majority of the answers given by the students concentrated in the range of three to five, affirming what was already expected, that the acceptance of the use of the Robocode tool to help understand the concepts of object-oriented programming in web programming courses is very favorable.

In the question specifically addressing the perception of the effectiveness of students learning new programming skills using Robocode, the following results were obtained, as shown in Table 3.

Table 3. Perceived effectiveness of learning new programming skills

Question	Frequency	Percentage
It's increased a lot	12	30,77%
Increased a little	24	61,54%
It stayed the same	3	7,69%
Total	39	100%

According to table 3, more than 90% of the participants reported that their programming skills had increased as a result of taking part in the Robocode championship. Among these participants, more than 30% said that their skills had improved significantly and more than 60% reported that their skills had increased reasonably. Only less than 10% reported that their skills remained the same. This result strongly suggests that Robocode was effective in promoting self-motivated learning.

Finally, the average grades of the students in the web programming I course from the previous year when the Robocode tool was not used (group 1) were compared with the average grades in the web programming I course when the Robocode tool was used (group 2).

The t-test with independent samples was used to compare the means. The results obtained with the Action tool are shown in figure 9 below.

Informação	Valor
T	-2,808248435
Graus de Liberdade	6
P-valor	0,030827191
Média no grupo 1:	4,125
Média no grupo 2:	7,175
Desvio padrão amostral do grupo 1:	1,31497782
Desvio padrão amostral do grupo 2:	1,728920665
Desvio padrão agrupado:	1,535957899
Hipótese Alternativa: Diferente de	0
Intervalo de Confiança	95%
Limite Inferior	-5,707557306
Limite Superior	-0,392442694

Figure 9. Results of the t-test with independent samples

We can see in figure 9 that in the previous year, the average grade for web programming I (group 1) was 4.1. However, with the Robocode championship, the average for the web programming I subject (group 2) was 7.2. This reinforces the suggestion that the Robocode tool applied to promote learning really is effective.

CONCLUSION

The activities applied and developed in this work facilitate teaching and learning and encourage students to stay on the course.

It was observed that the activities involving the Robocode software are valid for those who wish to learn or improve their knowledge of programming. The Robocode championship motivated students to continue in the course, reduced the number of failures in the programming subject and reduced the number of dropouts from the Information Systems course.

Based on the results obtained, it can be considered that, from the students' point of view, Robocode can be a way of forcing students to develop new skills and logical reasoning, increase their learning capacity, improve their knowledge of Object-Oriented Programming, encourage and motivate their studies and learning. In addition, Robocode can be a tool that, from the students' point of view, can help programming students who have difficulties learning Object-Oriented Programming, making it more fun and interesting through real practical activities.

In addition to the considerations mentioned above, this type of activity is an opportunity to change the tiring routine of programming classes and, in addition to interactive and fun learning, to encourage students to socialize in the school environment. In addition, it was found that there was greater interaction between the students and the teacher and between the students themselves, one helping the other and this collegial relationship facilitates and contributes to mutual learning. The students feel challenged by the game, and seek to improve the concepts they have already studied, as well as looking for new concepts not yet covered in the classroom, in order to implement more competitive robots.

Robocode has made programming more fun, as it involves creating robots to fight in a virtual arena, but through a practical real-world activity. We also observed the development of new skills and logical reasoning, capacity, improvement of knowledge, encouragement and motivation to study and teamwork. It was concluded that the activity applied and developed in this article is a tool that can facilitate the teaching and learning of students regardless of their level of education.

At the end of this work, it can be seen that Robocode is a tool that can help students in web programming I and II who have difficulties in Object-Oriented Programming.

With Robocode, programming becomes more fun, as you create robots to fight in a virtual arena, but through a real-world activity.

Robocode allowed students to apply their knowledge of Object-Oriented Programming, stimulate creativity and participation in group work, code robots using notions of physics and geometry, put into practice what is studied and discussed in the classroom, stimulate creativity and acceptance of new challenges by exploring teamwork and competitiveness.

The study met the proposed objective, which was to demonstrate that Robocode can help in the teaching and learning of the web programming I and II subjects, in which the content of Object-Oriented Programming is taught.

Finally, what has been covered in this work can help students and teachers in the area of programming, as it has covered several important concepts for this area and can serve as a basis for the development of future work.

As a suggestion for future work, we suggest expanding the research to include a larger number of students from technical and higher technology courses on different campuses or institutions and using more free tools such as Robocode.

REFERENCES

AMARAL, A. L. The eternal crossroads: how to select paths for higher education teacher training. In: XXII ENDIPE, 2004, Curitiba. Local knowledge and universal knowledge: research, didactics and teaching action. Belo Horizonte: Editora Universitària Champangnat. v. 1, p. 139150. 2004.

AMARAL, L. R.; SILVA, G. B.; PANTALEÂO, E. Robocode Platform as a Playful Tool for Teaching Computer Programming - University Extension in Public Schools of Minas Gerais. In: Proceedings of the XXVI Brazilian Symposium on Informatics in Education - SBIE, 2015.

BATISTA, G. Design e Educaçâo: o jogo no desenvolvimento de competências e habilidades do educando. Rio de Janeiro, 2010. Available at :<http://www2.dbd.puc-rio.br/pergamum/tesesabertas/0812129_10_pretextual.pdf >. Accessed October 2014.

BITTENCOURT, R. A. et al. Learning Programming through Playful Environments in a Computer Engineering Course: A First Incursion. WEI - XXI Workshop on Computing Education, p. 749 - 758. 2013.

BONAKDARIAN, E.; WHITE, L. Robocode throughout the curriculum. Journal of Computing Sciences in Colleges, v.19, n.3, p.311-313, 2004.

CABRAL, M. I. C. et al. Profile of computer science and informatics courses in Brazil, XXVII SBC Congress - XV WEI, Rio de Janeiro, 2007.

CUNHA, M. B. Games in chemistry teaching: theoretical considerations for their use in the classroom. QUiMICA NOVA NA ESCOLA. v. 34, n. 2, p. 9298, May 2012.

CZAJKOWSKI, A.; PATAN, K. Real-Time Learning of Neural Networks and its Application to the Prediction of Opponent Movement in the Robocode Enviroment. XI International PhD Workshop. Conference Archives. 2009.

DIAS, K. L.; SERRAO, M. S. A Linguagem Scratch no Ensino de Programaçâo: Um Relato de Experiência com Alunos Iniciantes do Curso de Licenciatura em Computação. In: XXII Workshop on Computer Education, Brasilia. Social Systems and Mass Events: Expanding Computing Challenges. 2014.

FARDO, M. L. Gamification as a pedagogical strategy: a study of game elements applied to teaching and learning processes. Master's dissertation, Universidade Caxias do Sul, Postgraduate Program in Education, 2013: Available at: https://repositorio.ucs.br/jspui/bitstream/11338/457/1/Dissertacao%20Marcelo %20Luis%20Fardo.pdf. Accessed in October 2014.

FRANÇA, R. S.; SILVA, W. C; AMARAL, H. J. C. "Computino: um jogo destinado à aprendizagemde Números Binàrios para estudantes da educaçâo bàsica". In Anais do XXXIII Congresso da SBC- WEI. Maceió, Brazil. 2013.

FREITAS, R. L.; PIVA JR, D. Strategies to improve abstraction processes in the discipline of Algorithms. In: XIX Workshop on Computing Education, Natal, RN. 2011.

GADE, M. et al. Applying Machine Learning to Robocode. JSK, Aalborg University, Aalborg, 2003.

HARPER, R. Co-evolving Robocode tanks. In: 13th annual conference on Genetic and evolutionary computation (GECCO '11), New York, USA. Proceedings... ACM, p.1443-1450, 2011.

HARTNESS, K. Robocode: using games to teach artificial intelligence. Journal of Computing Sciences in Colleges archive. Volume 19. pp. 287-291. 2004.

KAPP, K. M. The Gamification of Learning and Instruction: Game-based methods and strategies for training and education. San Francisco: Pfeiffer. 2012.

KENSLER, J. A.; AGAH, A. Neural networks-based adaptive bidding with the contract net protocol in multi-robot systems. Applied Intelligence, v. 31, n.3, 2009.

LIMA, A. F.; ARAUJO, M. N.; PINTO, V. P.; PAIVA, A. T. S. Educational Robotics Using Robocode as a Teaching Tool to Reduce Student Dropout in the Electrical Engineering Course. In: Brazilian Congress of Engineering Education - COBENGE, 2014, Juiz De Fora - MG. 2014.

LIU, P. L. Using open-source Robocode as a Java programming assignment. SIGCSE Bull, n.40, v.4, p.63-67, 2008.

LOBO ROBERTO, et al. Evasion in Brazilian Higher Education. Caderno de Pesquisa do Instituto Lobo para o Desenvolvimento da Educaçao, da Ciência e da Tecnologia. Sao Paulo, v. 37, n. 132, p. 641-659, 2007.

LONG, J. Just for Fun: Using Programming Games in Software Programming Training and Education - A Field Study of IBM Robocode Community, Journal of Information Technology Education, Vol. 6, p-279-290, 2007.

MARTINS, E. R. Using Robocode as a Tool to Assist the Teaching of Object-Oriented Programming in the Web Programming Discipline. Technical and Technological Journal: Science, Technology, Society, v. 1, p. 1-8, 2015.

MARTINS, E. R. Using Robocode as a Tool to Help Teach Object-Oriented Programming. In: II Escola Regional de Informàtica de Goiàs, Goiânia: Gràfica UFG, v. 1, p. 183-188, 2014.

MATTAR, J. "Games in education: how digital natives learn", In: Pearson Prentice Hall, Sâo Paulo, 2010.

MORAN, J. M. Integration of Technologies in Education. In: Leap into the Future. Brasilia: Posigraf. 2005.

MORAN, J. M. The education we want: New challenges and how to get there. 4. ed. Sâo Paulo: Papirus. 2009.

MORAN, J. M.; MASETTO, M. T.; BEHRENS, M. A. (Ed.). New technologies and pedagogical mediation. 13. ed. Sâo Paulo: Papirus. 2007.

NICOLETTI, A. A. M; FILHO, R. R. G. Aprender brincando: a utilização de jogos, brinquedos e brincadeiras como recurso pedagógico. Revista de divulgaçâo técnico-cientifica do ICPG, v. 2, n.5, p. 91-94, 2004.

O'KELLY, J.; GIBSON, J. P. RoboCode & problem-based learning: a non- prescriptive approach to teaching programming. SIGCSE Bull, n.38, v.3, p.217-221, 2006.

ROBOCODE. Read to me Robocode. Available at: http://robocode.sourceforge.net/docs/ReadMe.html. Accessed October 2015.

SANTOS, C. S.; SANTOS, A. H. M.; SOUZA, S. M.; SANTOS, D. M. B.; BITTENCOURT, R. A. Learning Object-Oriented Programming with a Playful Approach Based on Greenfoot and Robocode. In: XLIII Brazilian Congress of Engineering Education - COBENGE, 2015.

SAVI, R.; ULBRICHT, V. R. Educational Digital Games: Benefits and Challenges. RENOTE - Revista Novas Tecnologias na Educaçâo. v.6, n. 2, p.110. 2008.

SILVA, F. C. L. A tool for teaching artificial intelligence using computer games. 2007. Dissertaçâo (Master of Science) - Instituto de Matemàtica e Estatistica da Universidade de Sâo Paulo, University of Sâo Paulo, Sâo Paulo, 2007.

SILVA, V. DO N.; NASCIMENTO, M. N. Investigation of the improvement of high school students' learning through the use of programming, robotics and digital games. XI SBGames, 2012.

SILVEIRA, I.J.; ESMIN, A.A.A. AVA - Um ambiente Visual para a construção de algoritmos, 3rd International Conference on Engineering and Computer Education, Sâo Paulo, 2003.

TPE. In 2012, 1.6 million children and adolescents dropped out of school. Available at: http://www.todospelaeducacao.org.br/educacao-na- media/indice/27260/in-2012-16-million-children-and-adolescents-dropped-out-of-school/ Accessed October 2014.

WIDEMAN, H.. et al. Unpacking the potential of educational gaming: a new tool for gaming research. Simulation & Gaming, Thousand Oaks, v. 38, n. 1, p. 10-30, 2007. Available at <http://www.yorku.ca/~rowston/unpacking.pdf>. Accessed October 2014.

WOOLLEY, B. G.; PETERSON, G. L. Unified Behavior Framework for Reactive Robot Control. Journal of Intelligent and Robotic Systems, v.55 n.2- 3, p.155-176, 2009.

YIN, R. K. Case Study: Planning and Methods. Porto Alegre: Bookman, 2005.

Printed by Books on Demand GmbH, Norderstedt / Germany